PIANO • VOCAL • GUITAR

SHAWN MENDES

WONDER

ISBN 978-1-70513-222-7

Visit Hal Leonard Online at
www.halleonard.com

Contact us:
Hal Leonard
7777 West Bluemound Road
Milwaukee, WI 53213
Email: info@halleonard.com

In Europe, contact:
Hal Leonard Europe Limited
42 Wigmore Street
Marylebone, London, W1U 2RN
Email: info@halleonardeurope.com

In Australia, contact:
Hal Leonard Australia Pty. Ltd.
4 Lentara Court
Cheltenham, Victoria, 3192 Australia
Email: info@halleonard.com.au

contents

INTRO

Words and Music by SHAWN MENDES,
TOBIAS JESSO JR. SCOTT HARRIS
and ADAM FEENEY

WONDER

Words and Music by SHAWN MENDES,
THOMAS HULL, SCOTT HARRIS
and NATE MERCEREAU

C♯m
4fr
A
wonder, would-n't it be nice to live in-side a world that
E
is-n't black and white? I wonder what it's like to be my friends,
F♯m
C♯m
4fr
hope that they don't think I for-get a-bout them. I won-der,
A
I won-der.

E
F♯m
Right be - fore I close my eyes, the on - ly thing that's on my mind. Been
C♯m
4fr
A
Am
N.C.
dream - ing that you feel it too, I won - der what it's like to be loved by
E
F♯m
you. Yeah. I won-der what it's like.
C♯m
4fr
A
To Coda
I won - der what it's like to be loved by...

E
F♯m
Won - der why I'm so a - fraid of say - ing some-thing wrong, I nev - er
C♯m
4fr
said I was a saint. I won - der when I'm cry - ing in my hands, I'm con -
A
E
di-tioned to feel like it makes me less of a man. And I won - der if some day you'll
F♯m
be by my side and tell me that the world will end up al - right.

C♯m
4fr
A
Am
D.S. al Coda
I won - der,
I won - der.
CODA
like to be loved by you.
N.C.
E
F♯m
C♯m
4fr
A
E
I won-der what it's like to be loved by you.

F♯m
C♯m
4fr
Yeah. I won-der what it's like to be loved by you, yeah.
A
E
I won - der what it's like to be loved by... Right be - fore I
F♯m
C♯m
4fr
close my eyes, the on - ly thing that's on my mind. Been dream - ing that you
3
A
E
feel it too. I won - der what it's like to be loved by you.

HIGHER

Words and Music by SHAWN MENDES
and SCOTT HARRIS

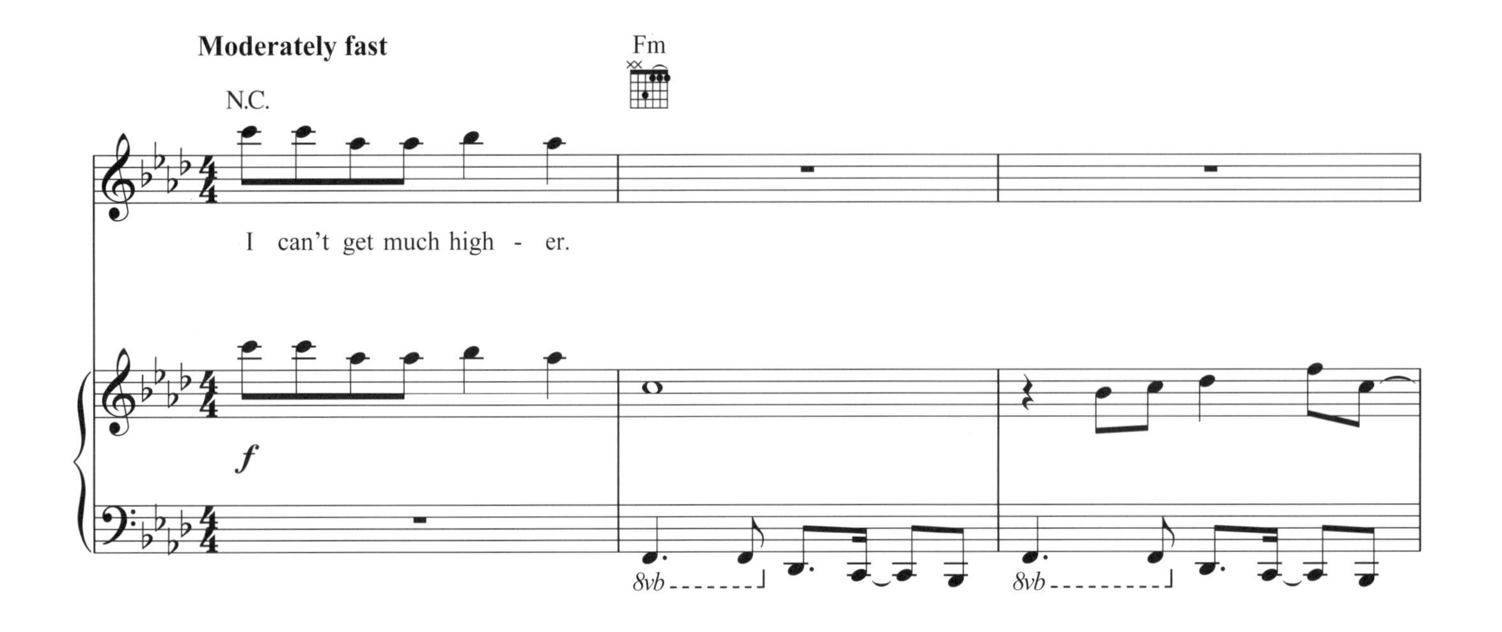

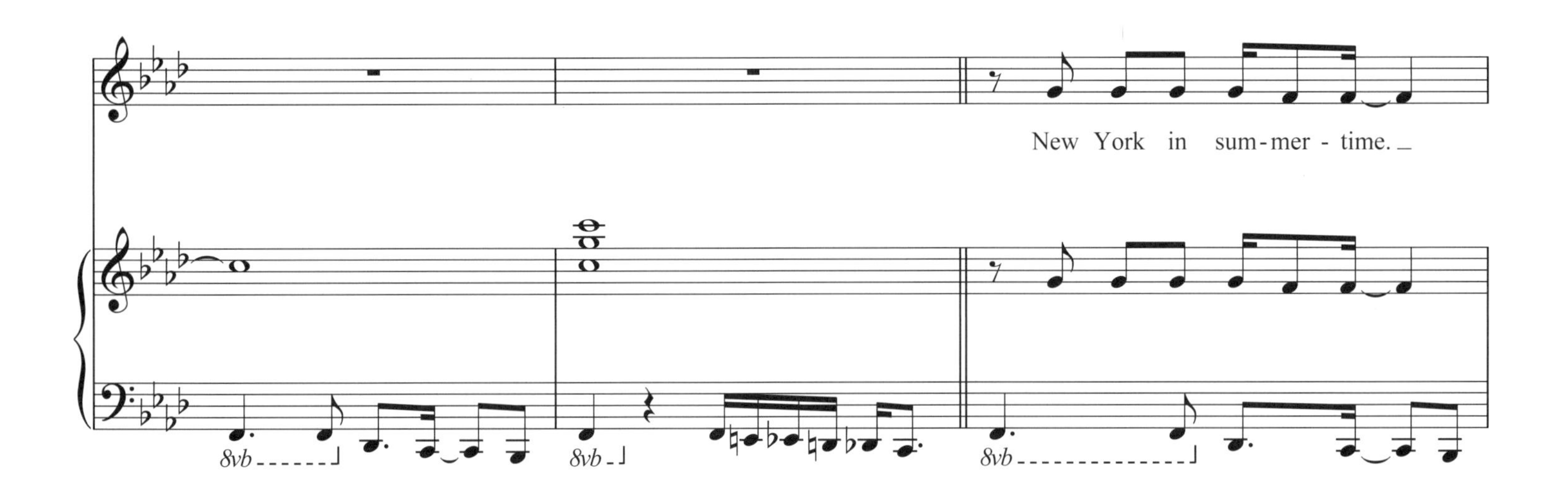

B♭m
Last year was a bro-ken heart.
Last year was a bro-ken heart. Damn,
8vb
Cm7
3fr
Fm
flip it a-round: what a beau-ti-ful start.
You and me on the top of the roof,
8vb
slow dance in the light of the moon.
Nev-er thought I would get this far.
8vb
8vb
B♭5
Nev-er thought I would get this far, no.
Nev-er thought I would get this far. Wow,
8vb

Cm
3fr
Fm
flip it a - round: what a beau - ti - ful start. The drinks are get - ting bet - ter, the
8vb
food is look - ing nice. As long as we're to - geth - er, no,
8vb
8vb
B♭5
I can't get much high - er. I, I, no,
8vb
C5
3fr
Fm
I can't get much high - er. Let's stay like this for - ev - er. I'll
8vb

kiss you ev - 'ry night. As long as we're to - geth - er, no,
8vb
To Coda
B♭5
C5
3fr
I can't get much high - er. I, I, no, I can't get much high - er.
Fm
N.C.
All eyes are look-ing at us, but I can't stop fall-ing in love.

Al - ways been the one that I want. _ Al - ways been the one that I want. _
8vb
B♭5
C5
3fr
Al - ways been the one that I want. _ Wow, look at us now. _ Damn, what have I done? _
Fm
I al - most can't be - lieve it, so please don't wake me if I'm
B♭m7
Cm7
3fr
D.S. al Coda
dream - ing. When - ev - er I'm with you... ___ The

CODA
N.C.
Fm
I can't get much high - er. Say,
say you won't let
go.
All I
B♭m7
know
is that
C5
3fr
I can't get much high - er.
N.C.
I can't get much high - er.
The drinks are get - ting bet - ter,
Fm
the
food is look - ing nice.
As long as we're to - geth - er,
no,
8vb

B♭5
C5
3fr
I can't get much high - er. I, I, no, I can't get much high - er. Let's
Fm
stay like this for - ev - er. I'll kiss you ev - 'ry night. As long as we're to - geth - er, no,
8vb
B♭5
C5
3fr
I can't get much high - er. I, I, no, I can't get much high - er.
8vb
Fm
N.C.
(8vb)
8vb

CALL MY FRIENDS

Words and Music by SHAWN MENDES, THOMAS HULL, SCOTT HARRIS, NATE MERCEREAU and JOHN HENRY RYAN

G
C
D
Cm6
3fr
Have-n't seen your fac - es in a while.
I should call my friends.
C5
B5
A5
D5
5fr
I should call my friends and go get high.
I need a va - ca - tion from my
mind.
I wan - na go. No - bod - y knows me bet - ter
E5
F♯5
G5
than them.
Wan - na feel some - thing a - gain.
I should call my friends.
To Coda

Cmaj9
Am11
3fr
D(add4)
I don't wan-na miss an-oth-er birth-day.
Feels like it's been for-ev-er since nine-teen.
I just wan-na be right where you are.
I miss how it was when we wished we were old-er.
Feel-ing so far, and I wan-na be clos-er.
D.S. al Coda

CODA
Cmaj7
G/B
Am9
5fr
Ooh, I know you got - ta make some sac - ri - fic - es.
Cmaj7
G/B
Em7
Am9
5fr
Ooh, don't wan - na be a - lone for one more night.
Cmaj7
G/B
Am9
5fr
Ooh, I know you got - ta make some sac - ri - fic - es. But
Cm6
3fr
C5
3fr
B5
A5
5fr
D5
5fr
I should call my friends.
I should call my friends.

C5
B5
A5
D5
3fr
5fr
I should call my friends and go get high.
I need a va - ca - tion from my mind.
E5
F♯5
G5
I wan - na go. No - bod - y knows me bet - ter than them.
Wan - na
feel some - thing a - gain.
I should call my friends.

24 HOURS

Words and Music by SHAWN MENDES,
THOMAS HULL, SCOTT HARRIS
and NATE MERCEREAU

N.C.
I don't know_ how this-'ll go._ I prom-ise that_ I love you so._ I'll
bet it all_ on me and you. I'll bet it all, you're bul-let-proof. Let's
F C/F F6 Fmaj7
3fr
throw a-way_ our back-up plans,_ and peo-ple might_ not un-der-stand._ Who
B♭maj7 B♭
cares a-bout if they ap-prove? I'd face them all_ to be with you._

F
C/E
Dm
C
All it'd take is twen-ty-four hours.
all it'd take is twen-ty-four hours.
Sign the check and the place is
B♭
Dm/A
B♭
F/C
ours. It's a lit-tle soon, but I wan-na come home to you.
F
C/E
Dm
C
All it'd take is twen-ty-four hours. We could dance, you could throw the
B♭
Dm/A
B♭
F/C
To Coda
flow-ers. It's a lit-tle soon, but I wan-na come home to you. I

N.C.
heard that once a wise man said, "On-ly fools go rush-ing in." But I'm
F/C
not the type to o-ver-think when some-thing feels so right. And I
F
F/E
Dm
C
prom-ise I'll mean ev-'ry word. I'll paint the world that you de-serve. Ev-'ry
B♭
B♭/A
B♭
Csus
3fr
D.S. al Coda
col-or you'd im-ag-ine. I can't wait for it to hap-pen, 'cause

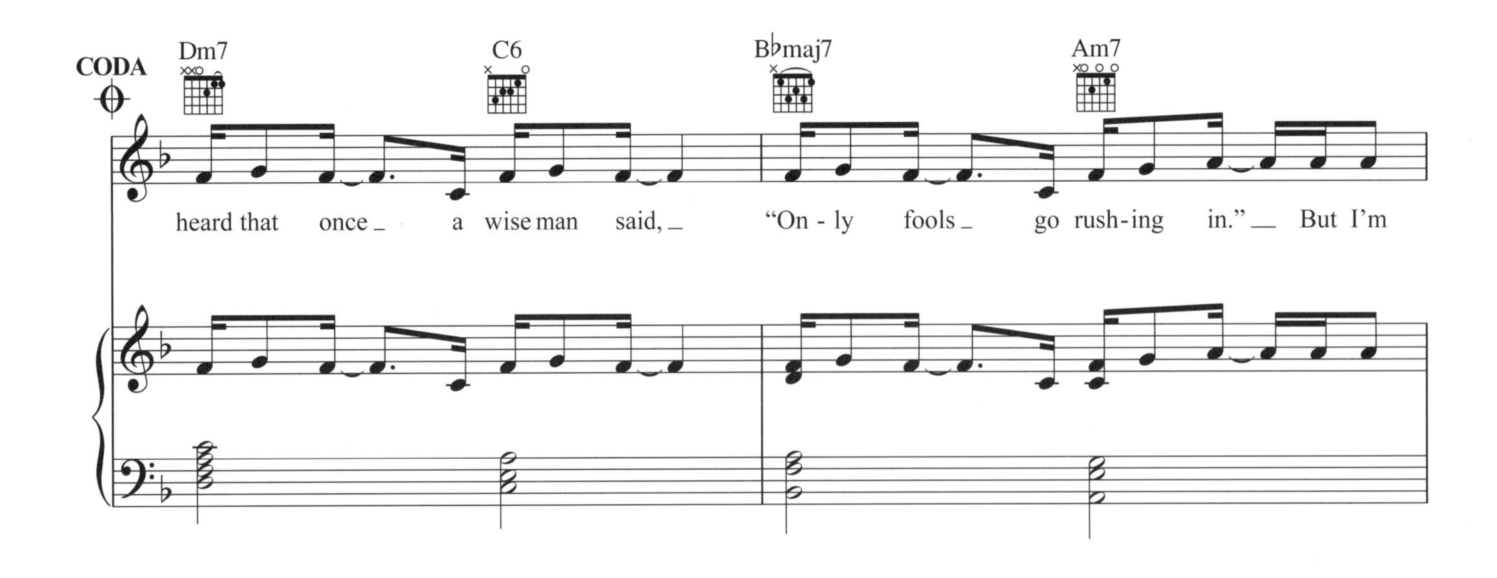
CODA
Dm7
C6
B♭maj7
Am7
heard that once a wise man said, "On - ly fools go rush-ing in." But I'm

G9
9fr
not the type to o - ver - think. I'm not the type to o - ver - think.

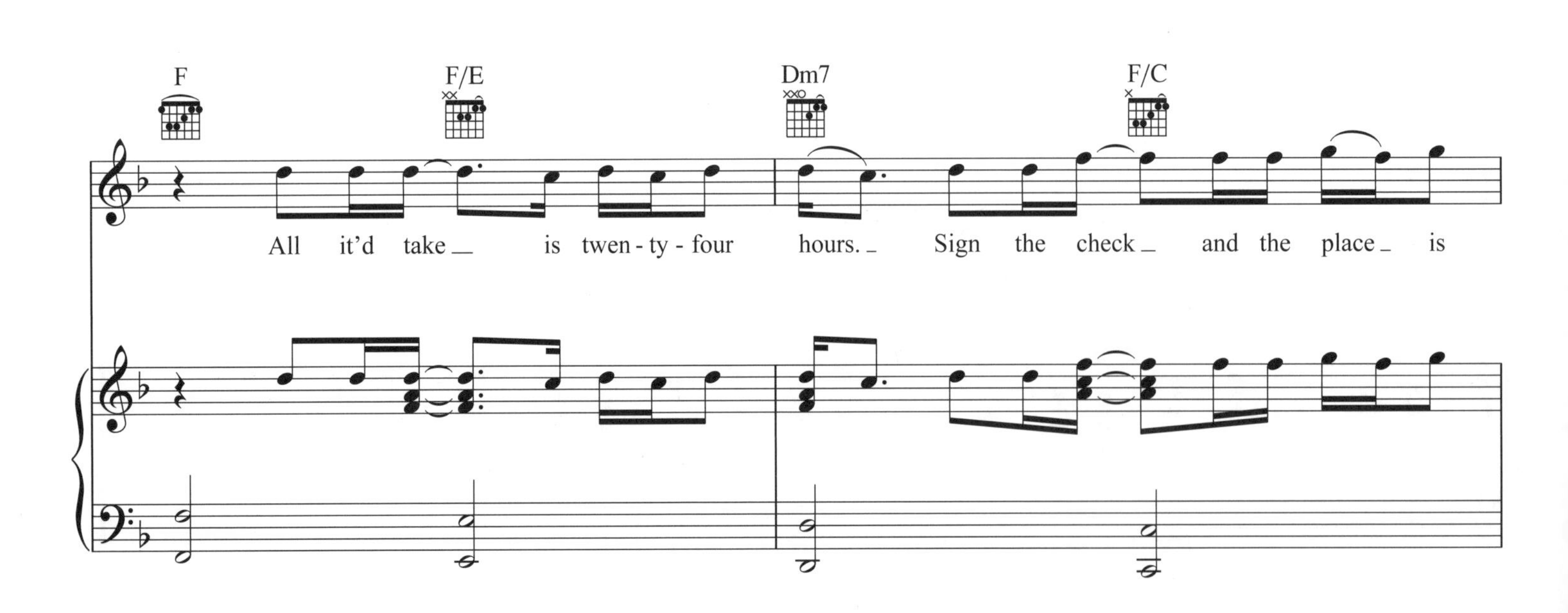
F
F/E
Dm7
F/C
All it'd take is twen - ty - four hours. Sign the check and the place is

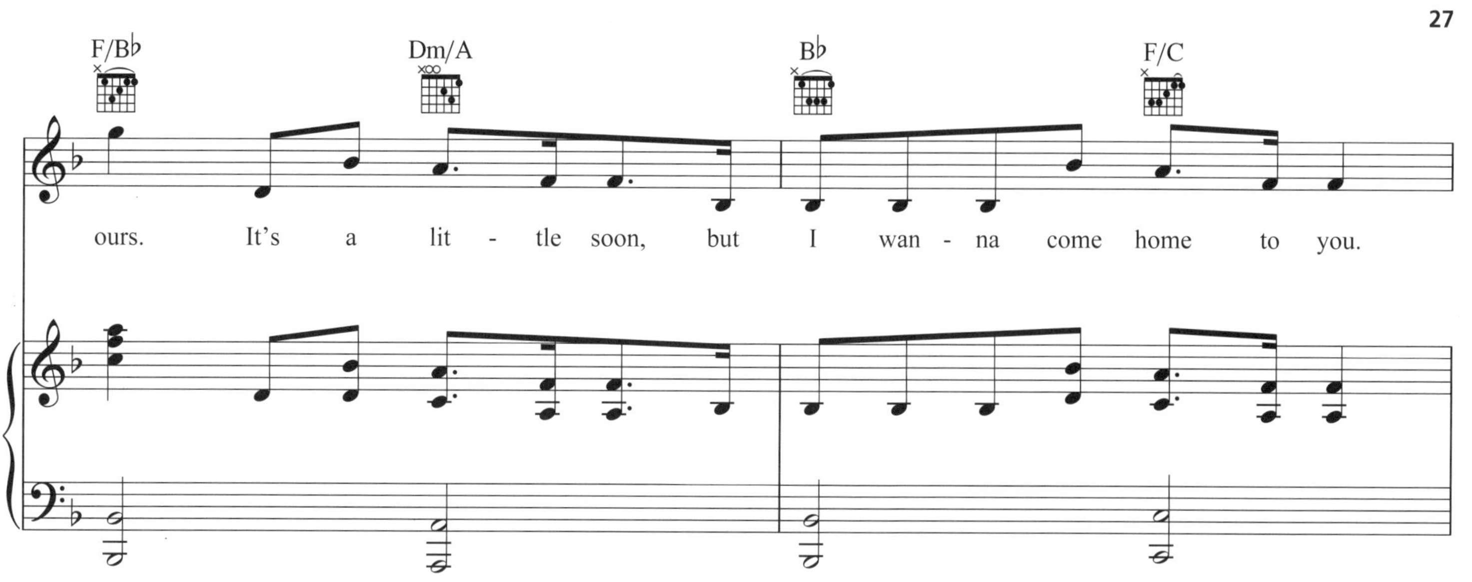
F/B♭
Dm/A
B♭
F/C
ours. It's a lit - tle soon, but I wan - na come home to you.

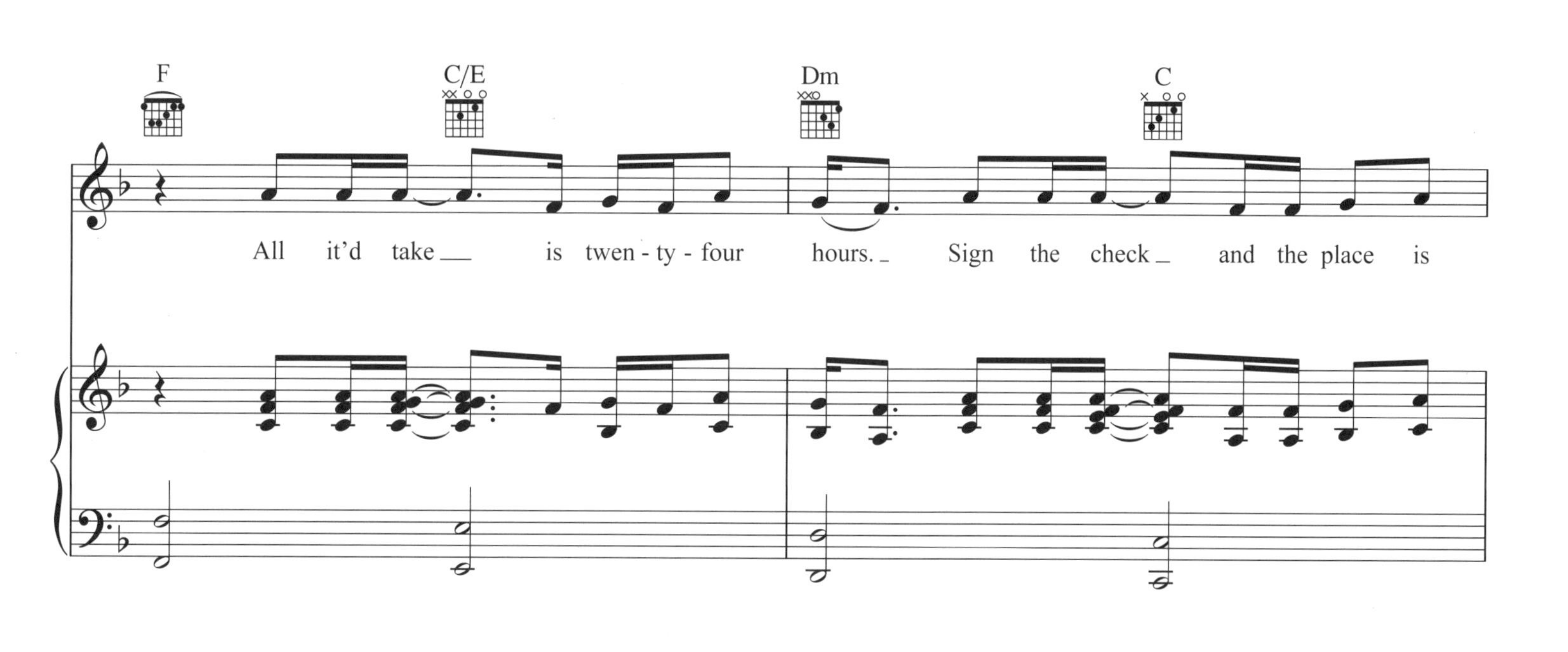
F
C/E
Dm
C
All it'd take is twen - ty - four hours. Sign the check and the place is

B♭
Dm/A
B♭
F/C
N.C.
ours. It's a lit - tle soon, but I wan - na come home to you.
8va

TEACH ME HOW TO LOVE

Words and Music by SHAWN MENDES,
THOMAS HULL, SCOTT HARRIS
and NATE MERCEREAU

Cmaj7
Em7
F
you. Won't you draw a map for me
Dm7
F
laced with straw - ber - ries, and I'll get on my knees.
E
Am7
Dm7
Put my hands a - round you. Ooh, teach me how to
G6
C
Em7
touch you, tease, ca - ress you and please you. Teach me how to love.

Am7 Dm7

Put my hands a - round you. Ooh, teach me how to

G6 C Em7

touch you, tease, ca - ress you and please you. Teach me, teach me, teach me how to love.

Am7 Dm7 G

Your im - ag - i - na - tion. Now I'm fix - at - ed, and I'm dy - ing

C Em7 Am7 Dm7

to learn. Ev - 'ry inch of you there's some - thing new,

G
C
Em7
Fmaj7
eff - ing me up. I'm what you de - serve. Just draw a map for me
Dm7
F6/B
laced with straw - ber - ries, and I'll get on my knees.
E
Am7
Dm7
Put my hands a - round you. Ooh, teach me how to
G6
C
Em7
touch you, tease, ca - ress you and please you. Teach me how to love.

Am7
Dm7
Put my hands a - round you. Ooh, teach me how to
G6
C
Em7
touch you, tease, ca - ress you and please you. Teach me, teach me, teach me how to love,
Am7
Dm7
G
how to love, how to love.
C
Em7
Am
Teach me, teach me, teach me how to love.

Am/D
Am/G
N.C.
Am7
Teach me, teach me teach me how to love.
(Babe, I won't stop 'til you feel the rush. Babe,
Dm7
1
G
I won't stop 'til you feel the rush. Babe, I won't stop 'til you feel the rush.)
C
Em7
2
G
Teach me, teach me, teach me how to love.
(Babe, I won't stop 'til you feel the rush.)

C6
Am7
Dm7
Put my hands a - round you. Ooh, teach me how to
G6
C
Em7
touch you, tease, ca - ress you and please you. Teach me how to love.
Am7
Dm7
Put my hands a - round you. Ooh, teach me how to
G6
C
Em7
touch you, tease, ca - ress you and please you. Teach me, teach me, teach me how to love,

Am7
Dm7
G
how to love,
how to love.
1
C
Em7
Teach me, teach me, teach me how to love.
2
C
Em7
Teach me, teach me, teach me how to love.
(Babe,
Am7
Dm7
G6
I won't stop 'til you feel the rush. Babe, I won't stop 'til you feel the rush. Babe, I won't stop 'til you feel the rush.)
1
C
Em7
Teach me, teach me, teach me how to love.
(Babe,
2
N.C.
Em7
Am
Teach me, teach me, teach me how to love.

DREAM

Words and Music by SHAWN MENDES,
THOMAS HULL, SCOTT HARRIS
and NATE MERCEREAU

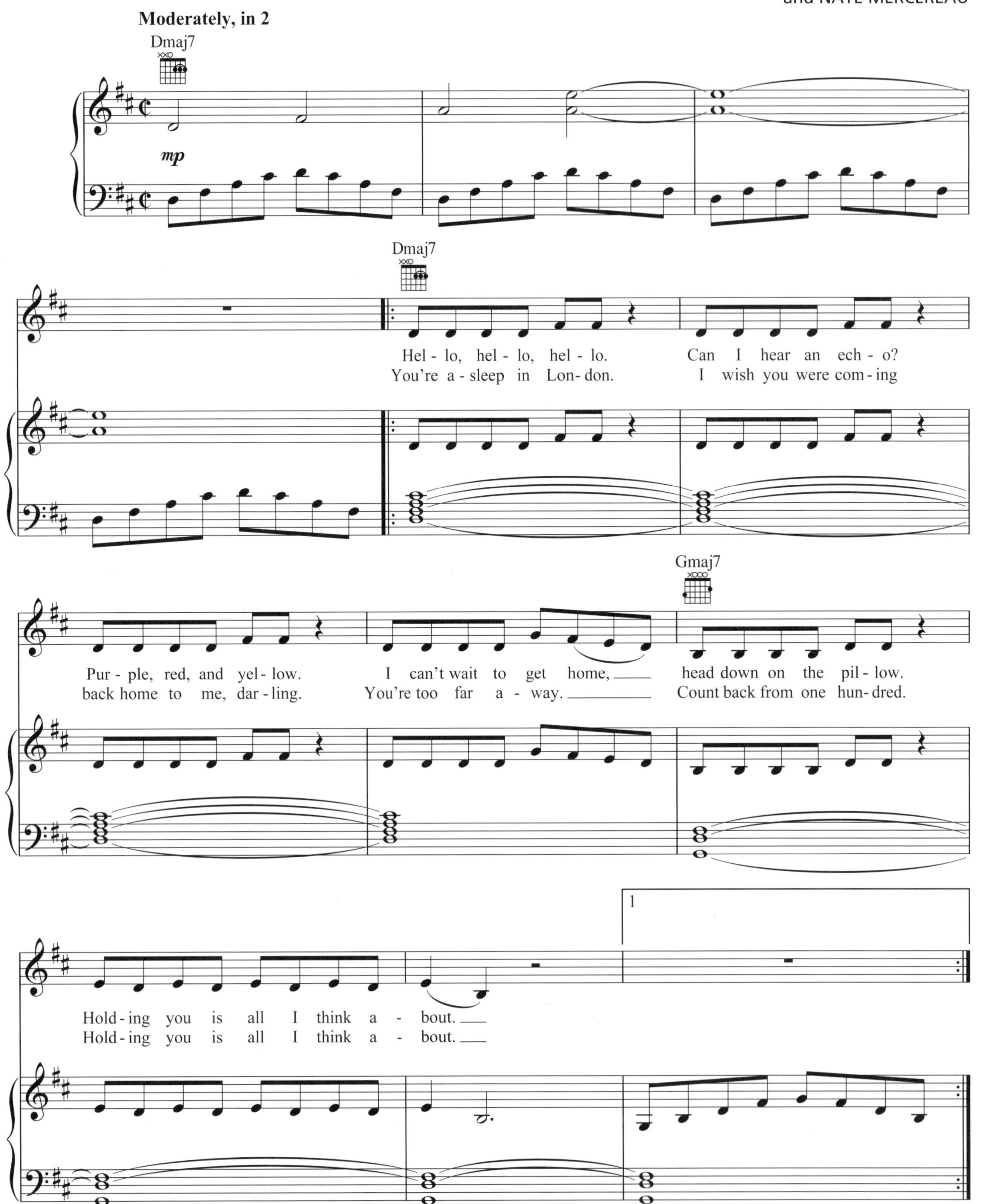

2
Am7
B7
Oh, ba - by, when I'm a - part from you,
Cmaj7
G
I just shut my eyes.
All I have to do
B7
Dmaj9
4fr
is dream, dream, dream, dream
1
Gmaj9
a - bout you,

2
Gmaj9
- you. (A - bout you, a - bout you, a - bout you, a - bout you.
A - bout you, a - bout you, a - bout you, a - bout you.)
D
Hel - lo, hel - lo, hel - lo.
Walk - ing through a mead - ow full of sun - flow - ers, pick - ing off the pet - als.
G
I don't wan - na wake up with - out you lay - ing next to me, yeah.

D
I'm no good at wait - ing. All this sep - a - ra - tion.
Feel - ing suf - fo - cat - ed. I just need to breathe.
N.C.
And
G
I'm start - ing to hate it. I can't wait to fall a - sleep.
Am7
Oh, ba - by, when I'm a - part from you,
B7

Cmaj7
G
I just shut my eyes, and all I have to do
B7
Dmaj9
is dream, dream, dream, dream
Gmaj9
a - bout you, (A - bout you, a - bout you,
a - bout you, a - bout you. A - bout you, a - bout you, a - bout you, a - bout you.)

Dmaj9
4fr
dream, dream, dream, dream a - bout
Gmaj9
you. (A - bout you, a - bout you, a - bout you, a - bout you. A - bout you, a - bout you,
Fmaj7♯11
a - bout you, a - bout you.)
8va
Fmaj7
(8va)
Cmaj7

B7
B
Dmaj9
4fr
Dream, dream, dream, dream a - bout
1
Gmaj9
you,
2
Gmaj9
- you.
rit.

305

Words and Music by SHAWN MENDES,
THOMAS HULL, SCOTT HARRIS
and NATE MERCEREAU

* Recorded a half step lower.

G5
3fr
E5
You're my sun - light on a rain - y day.
Would take my heart with you if you
E7
A5
5fr
walked a - way.
I'm a mess right now,
I'm a wreck right now.
I'm
D
Gmaj7
wait - ing for the mo - ment that you let me down.
If you cut the cord, I don't know
there's a door to heav - en, ba - by,
Em7
E7
what I'd do.
Don't wan - na sky - dive with - out my par - a - chute.
I'm a
you're the key.
And if I had to beg, I'd be on my knees.
Oh,

Am7
D7
mess right now, baby, help me out. I'm scared I'm gon-na wake up and you'll
please don't say an-y-thing has changed. You're the one I wan-na wake up next to
C
D
Bm7
let me down. This feel-ing does-n't fade, no mat-ter how hard that I
ev-'ry day.
C
D
G/B
try. I al-ways think a-bout it at the same time ev-'ry
Cm
3fr
Gmaj7
night. It's three-oh-five. I'm on a roll-er

Em7
Am7
coast - er ride,
hop - ing you don't change your mind.
D
E5/D
2fr
D
I don't wan - na let go, I've nev - er been so sure in my life. I'm
3
Gmaj7
Em7
ter - ri - fied you'll turn a - round and say good - bye.
Am7
Hop - ing you don't change your mind. I don't wan - na let go, I've

D
1
E5/D
2fr
D
N.C.
nev - er been so sure in my life. If
2
E5/D
D
Cmaj7
Em
life. (I want to
Gmaj7/D
be with you. I want to fly with you.
C♯m7♭5
4fr
Cmaj7
I want to be with you, my love.)

Gmaj7
It's three - oh - five. I'm on a roll - er
Em7
Am7
coast - er ride, hop - ing you don't change your mind.
D
N.C.
I don't wan - na let go, I've nev - er been so sure. I'm
Gmaj7
Em7
ter - ri - fied you'll turn a - round and say good - bye.

Am7
Hop - ing you don't change your mind.
I don't wan - na let go, I've
D
E5/D
2fr
D
Gmaj7
nev - er been so sure in my life.
(I want to
3
Em7
Am7
be with you.
I want to fly with you.
I want to
D
Em/D
D
G
be with you, my love.)

SONG FOR NO ONE

Words and Music by SHAWN MENDES,
SCOTT HARRIS, NATE MERCEREAU
and ADAM FEENEY

* *Recorded a half step lower.*

F6
F+
F
this is a song for no one.
This is a song for no one.
Get on a plane, fly to the most beau - ti - ful place you've ev - er been.

F
F+
F6
F+
Close my eyes: things are bet - ter in my dreams 'cause I'm with
B♭
B♭m
F
F+
some - one, some - one I a - dore.
F6
F+
F
F+
F6
F+
This is a song for no
F
F+
F6
F+
F
F+
one. I wrote this song

F6
F+
F
F+
F6
F+
for no one.
F
F+
F6
F+
Yes - ter - day I got pret - ty drunk, said some things that I should - n't of. Told
F
F+
F6
F+
you that I real - ly love you. You did not re - cip - ro - cate those feel -
B♭
B♭m
- ings. But that's o - kay; I'll be fine an - y - way.

Moderately, in 2
N.C.
F
C
Gm
3fr
Bb
I wrote this
song for no one.
I wrote this
song.

F
C
Gm
3fr
B♭
1
No, I wrote this
song for no - bod - y.
2

MONSTER

Words and Music by JUSTIN BIEBER,
SHAWN MENDES, MUSTAFA AHMED,
ADAM FEENEY and ASHTON SIMMONDS

Dm
Fill me up with con - fi - dence, I say what's in my chest.
C
Spill my words and tear me down un - til there's noth - ing left.
G/B
Re - ar - range the piec - es just to fit me with the rest.
B♭
But what if I, what if I
Dm
trip? What if I, what if I
C
fall? Then am I the
Gm
mon - ster?
3fr

B♭
Just let me know.
What if I, what if I
Dm
C
sin?
What if I, what if I break?
Then am I the
To Coda
Gm
3fr
B♭
mon - ster?
Just let me know,
yeah,
3
N.C.
yeah, yeah, yeah.
I was fif - teen when the world put me on a ped - es - tal.
I had

big dreams of do-ing shows and mak-ing mem-o-ries. Made some bad moves, tryin' to act cool, up-
set by their jeal-ous-y. Lift-ing me up, lift-ing me up,
Dm
C
and tear-ing me down, tear-ing me down. I take re-spon-si-bil-i-ty for
Bm7♭5
ev-'ry-thing I've done. Hold-ing it a-gainst me like you're the ho-ly one.

B♭
N.C.
Dm
I had a chip on my shoul - der, had to
C
let it go.
'cause un - for - give - ness keeps them in con - trol.
I came
Gm
3fr
B♭
in with good in - ten - tions, then I let it go.
And now I real - ly want to
N.C.
D.S. al Coda
know.
What if I, what if I
CODA
B♭
know.
(Oh, please, just let me know.)

Dm
C
La da da da da da.
La da da da da da da na.
Gm
3fr
B♭
1
La da da da da da.
La da da da da da da na.
2
da da da na.
Dm
C
Gm
3fr
B♭

ALWAYS BEEN YOU

Words and Music by SHAWN MENDES,
TOBIAS JESSO, SCOTT HARRIS
and ZUBIN THAKKAR

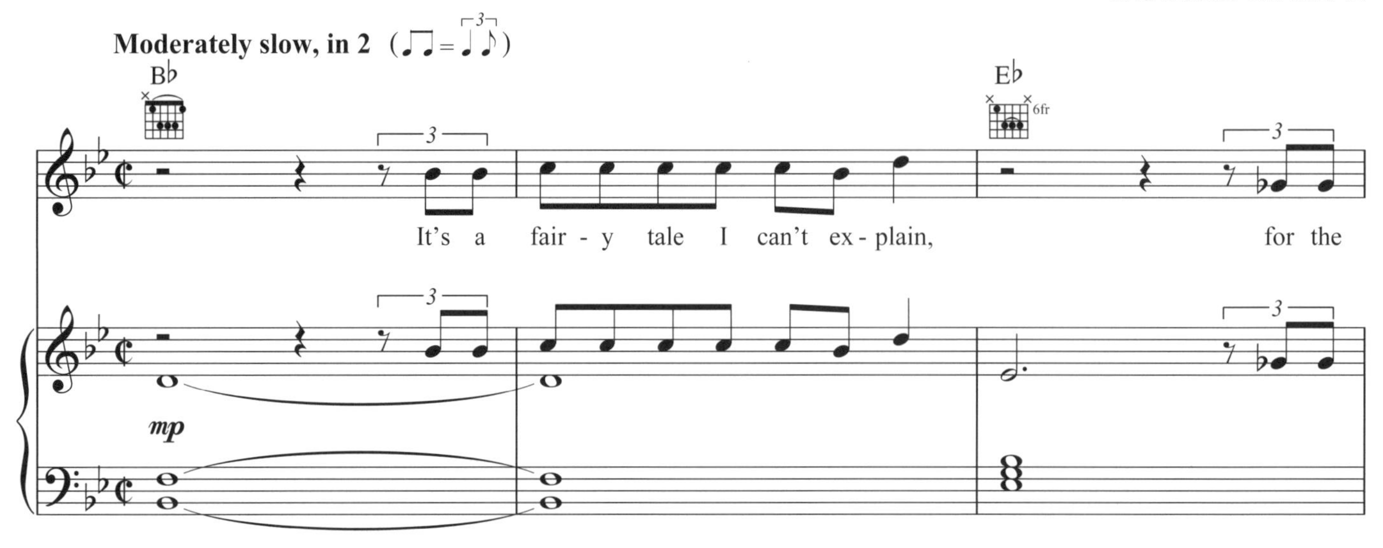

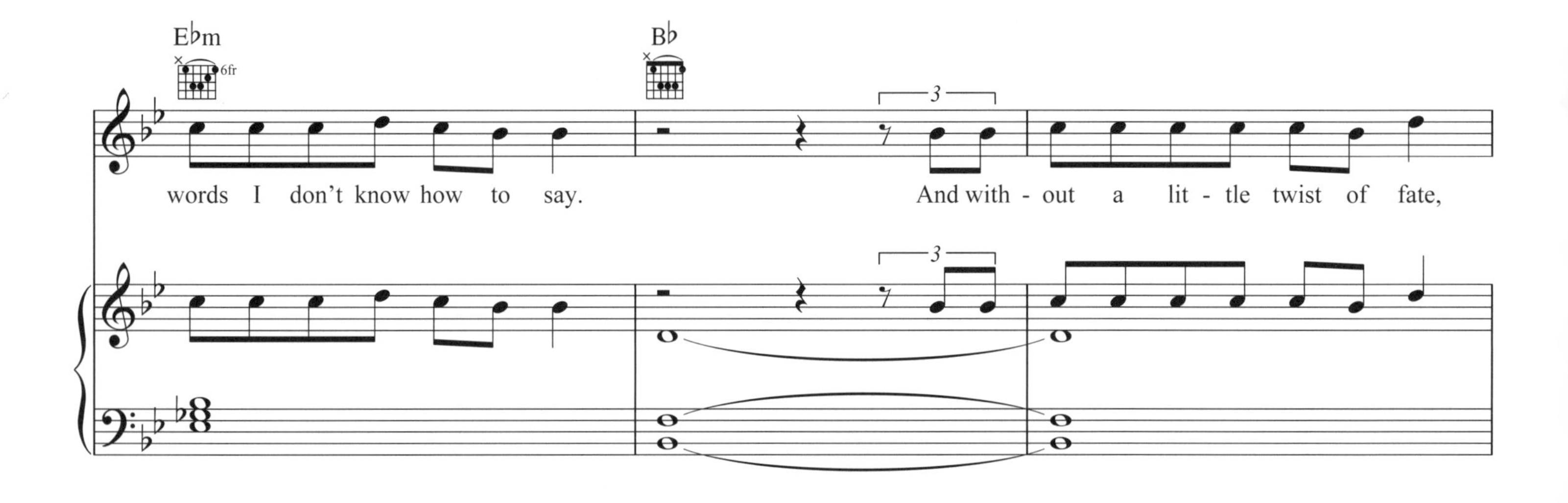

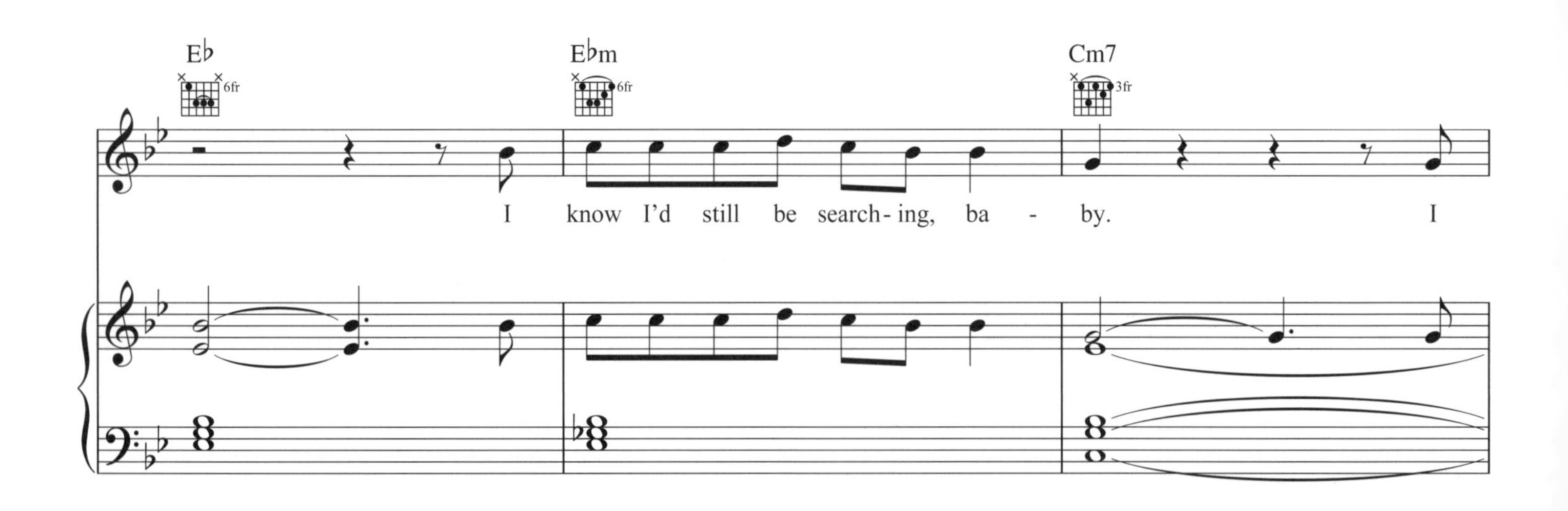

E♭maj9
6fr
E♭m6
swear that you've been sent to save me.
B♭
B♭/A
B♭/A♭
You're the on - ly one that my heart keeps com - ing back
E♭
6fr
E♭m
6fr
B♭
N.C.
3
to.
It's
ff
E♭
6fr
3
al - ways been you, it's al - ways been you.

E♭m
6fr
B♭
N.C.
It's al-ways been you, it's al-ways been you.
E♭
6fr
E♭m
6fr
Cm
3fr
E♭
6fr
To Coda
B♭
It's al - ways been you.
And
mp
you've seen all my dark - est fears,
E♭
6fr
like you've

E♭m7
6fr
B♭
known me for a thou - sand years.
The
E♭
6fr
3
boy who's real - ly un - der - neath,
or the
E♭m7
6fr
Cm7
3fr
scars and in - se - cu - ri - ties.
Ba - by,
I swear that you've been sent to save
E♭
6fr
E♭m7
6fr
B♭
me.
You're the on - ly

B♭/A
B♭/A♭
E♭
6fr
one that my heart keeps com - ing back to.
E♭m7
6fr
D.S. al Coda
CODA
B♭
B♭/A
You're the on - ly one that my heart
B♭/A♭
E♭
6fr
E♭m
6fr
keeps com - ing back to.
B♭
E♭
6fr
E♭m
6fr
(Ooh,

B♭
E♭
E♭m
6fr
Ooh, hoo, ooh.)
It's al - ways been you, yeah.
Cm
3fr
(Ah,
you.)
Straight eighths
Swing
B♭/A
It's al - ways been you.
You're the on - ly one that my heart
B♭/A♭
keeps com - ing back to.
N.C.

PIECE OF YOU

Words and Music by SHAWN MENDES,
SCOTT HARRIS, ERIC FREDERIC
and JOHN HENRY RYAN

* Recorded a half step higher.

D5
5fr
I get reck - less, I'm ob - ses - sive, I'm pa - thet - ic and pos - ses - sive.
You're so sure it makes me in - se - cure.
Dm
Dm(maj7)
Am/D
Dm6
You're ma - jes - tic, mes - mer - iz - ing; light the room up with - out try - ing.
B♭maj7/D
3fr
A/D
Ba - by, I'm so in - to you it hurts.

Dm Dm(maj7) Am/D Dm6 B♭maj7/D 3fr

Ah, it just is - n't fair. What you put in the air, I

N.C. Dm A/C♯ C6 Bm7♭5

don't wan - na share. Ev - 'ry - bod - y wants a piece of you.

B♭maj7 A

I get jeal - ous, but who would - n't when you look like you do?

Dm A/C♯ C6 Bm7♭5

From the sec - ond you walked in the room, my night is ru -

B♭maj7
Dm/A
A
N.C.
ined. Ev - 'ry - bod - y wants a piece. One, two, three.
D5
5fr
So do I. May - be I'm self - ish. Just one touch is so e - lec - tric.
Ev - 'ry lit - tle thing you do feels right, yeah. I'm
Dm
Dm(maj7)
Am/D
Dm6
sor - ry if I get pro - tec - tive. Need these boys to get the mes - sage.

B♭maj7/D
3fr
A/D
You know I'm yours, I know you're mine.
D5
5fr
N.C.
C♯5
4fr
C6
Bm7♭5
Ev - 'ry - bod - y wants a piece of you.
B♭6
A
I get jeal - ous, but who would - n't when you look like you do?
Dm
A/C♯
C6
Bm7♭5
From the sec - ond you walked in the room, my night is ru -

B♭maj7
Dm/A
N.C.
Dm11
3fr
ined. Ev - 'ry - bod - y wants a piece. It's so hard,
but it's true.
1
2
N.C.
Dm
C♯dim/E
Ev - 'ry - bod - y wants a piece. Ah, it
F
G
G♯dim7
just is - n't fair. What you put in the air, I

A
Dm
A/C♯
C6
Bm7♭5
don't wan - na share.
Ev - 'ry - bod - y wants a piece of you.
B♭maj7
A
Dm
A/C♯
I get jeal - ous, but who would-n't when you look like you do?
From the sec - ond you walked
C6
Bm7♭5
B♭maj7
Dm/A
A
in the room, my night is ru - ined.
Ev - 'ry - bod - y wants a piece.
Dm
C♯+
Fmaj7/C
Bm7♭5
B♭6
A

CAN'T IMAGINE

Words and Music by
SHAWN MENDES

F/A G C7
-ine what a world would be.
-ine what a world would be.
F F+ F
With - out you all the
With - out you I'd
F+ F F+
birds would stop their songs. With - out you
al - ways be a - lone. With - out you
F F+
all things right would feel so wrong.
I don't know where to go.

B♭m(maj7)
6fr
F/A
G
I can't im - ag - ine what a world would be.
C
F/B♭
F/A
No, I can't im - ag - ine what a
G
C
F/B♭
world could be.
I can't im - ag -
F/A
G
C7
- ine what a world would

F
F+
F
be.
F+
B♭m(maj7)
A+
6fr
I can't im - ag - ine.
B♭m(maj7)
F/A
F/B♭
6fr
I can't im - ag - ine, no, I can't im - ag -
F/A
G7
C7
- ine, no, what a world would be with - out
3
3

F
F+
F
you.
I'd
F+
F
F+
al - ways be ___ a - lone.
F
F+
F/B♭
I'd al - ways be ___ a - lone.
F/A
G7
C7
F
rit.

LOOK UP AT THE STARS

Words and Music by SHAWN MENDES,
THOMAS HULL and SCOTT HARRIS

D
Dmaj7
D6
D9
4fr
Be - fore you go home, I should let you know, I'm so glad that you came,
G/D
Bm/D
Em/D
A/D
D
Dmaj7
I know that we went late. But look up at the stars;
D6
D9
4fr
Gmaj7
Bm/F♯
Em
A6
they're like piec - es of art float - ing a - bove the ground. You
Bm
F♯7/A♯
4fr
D/A
E/G♯
G
know we could fly so far, the u - ni - verse is ours. I'm not gon - na let

Em
A
Fmaj7
you down.
I am feel - ing so
mf
Em7
Fmaj7
Em7
luck - y, (luck - y, luck - y, luck - y). The sun shin - ing down on me, (on me, on me, on me).
Fmaj7
Em7
A
To Coda
Got these an - gels all a - round me. I'll nev - er be a - lone.
D
Dmaj7
D6
A/D
Look up at the stars; they're like piec - es of art
f

G/D Bm/D Em A Bm F♯7/A♯
4fr
floating above the ground. You know we could fly so far,
D/A E/G♯ G Em A
the universe is ours, and I'm not gonna let you down.
D Dmaj7 D6 D9
4fr
mf
Finally we've met, now the lights are set. It's taken us till now
G/D Bm/D Em/D A/D
to be together in this town, yeah. A

D
Dmaj7
D6
D9
cou - ple of years we've been mak - ing plans, some - how you al - ways seem to un - der - stand. So,
G/D
Bm/D
Em
A
D.S. al Coda
let me spend the night in won - der - land with you.
CODA
D
D+
D6
D9
Look up at the stars; they're like piec - es of art
mp sub.
G
Bm/F♯
Em
A
Bm
F♯7/A♯
float - ing a - bove the ground. You know we could fly so far,
f

D/A
E/G♯
G
Em
A
the u-ni-verse is ours, and I'm not gon-na let you down.
D
Dmaj7
D6
A/D
G/D
Bm/D
Em
A
D
Dmaj7
Bm/D
A/D
G/D
Bm/D

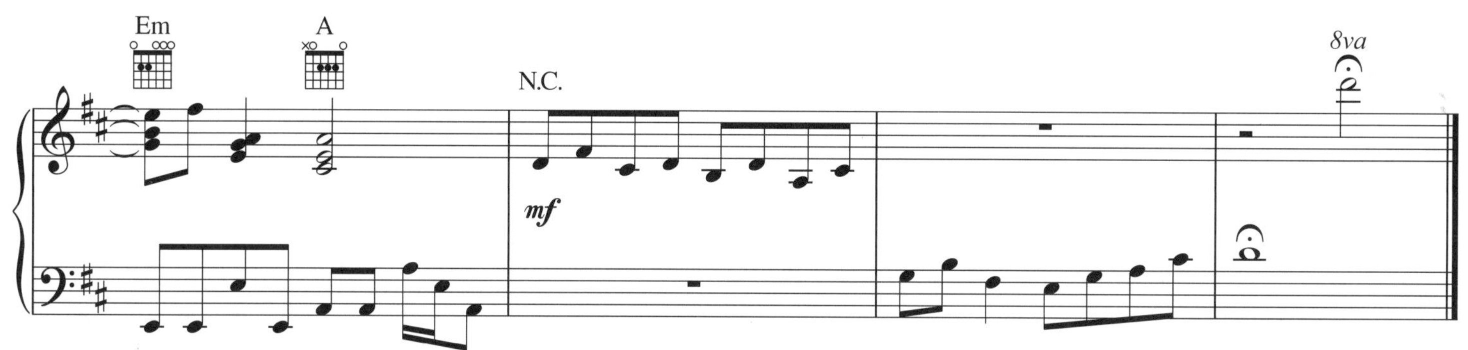
Em
A
N.C.
mf
8va